Corporate Tricks

Corporate Tricks

Margaret Polglase
Photography by Rob Henderson

NEW
HOLLAND

First published in Australia in 2004 by
New Holland Publishers (Australia) Pty Ltd
Sydney • Auckland • London • Cape Town

14 Aquatic Drive Frenchs Forest NSW 2086 Australia
218 Lake Road Northcote Auckland New Zealand
86 Edgware Road London W2 2EA United Kingdom
80 McKenzie Street Cape Town 8001 South Africa

National Library of Australia Cataloguing-in-Publication Data:

    Polglase, Margaret.
    Corporate tricks.

    ISBN 1 74110 132 8.

    1. Work environment. I. Henderson, Rob, 1945- . II. Title.

    650

Publishing Manager: Robynne Millward
Project Editor: Liz Hardy
Designer: Karlman Roper
Production Manager: Linda Bottari
Printer: Kyodo Printing, Singapore

10 9 8 7 6 5 4 3 2 1

When office politics get to you,
consult this book!

Margaret and Rob

If you can't get an office with a view …

try an office with a brew!

Once you get a foot in the door,

it's vital to make a good impression.

Start early.

Finish late.

Parking may be difficult.

You could waste time looking for a space.

Dress appropriately …

and be prepared for the unexpected!

Make sure there are no skeletons in your closet

that could come back to haunt you!

Be discreet

and avoid gossip.

If you air your dirty linen in public,

you could be banished!

It's simply not cricket

to boast about your conquests in the office.

Don't be a loner—

join in!

Be a team player,

and never sulk.

It's a balancing act

but it shouldn't weigh you down.

If you get that sinking feeling,

just try and keep your head above water.

Feel threatened?

Stay calm!

Something fishy going on?

Let the boss sort it out!

When the pressure builds,

get a move on!

Never lose your head

or you could end up looking ridiculous!

Look up to your superiors,

even if they seem intimidating.

It can be lonely at the top …

and cold!

There are barriers to break down,

and storms to weather.

There will be bridges to cross

and some will require courage.

Once your career gets off the ground,

we hope it soars!

Don't be afraid of falling …

you'll eventually get the hang of it.

For some, the climb is easy.

Others will need support.

Some days you'll work like a dog,

some days you'll look …!

After an office party,

help with the washing up.

If you are left to do the dirty work,

try to focus on the big picture.

Don't fish for compliments

or you could get a nasty surprise.

Travelling on company business?

Do it in style!

Stay in touch with the office,

no matter where you are.

If you have to speak at a conference,

be outstanding.

Keep your head out of the clouds

and your feet on the ground.

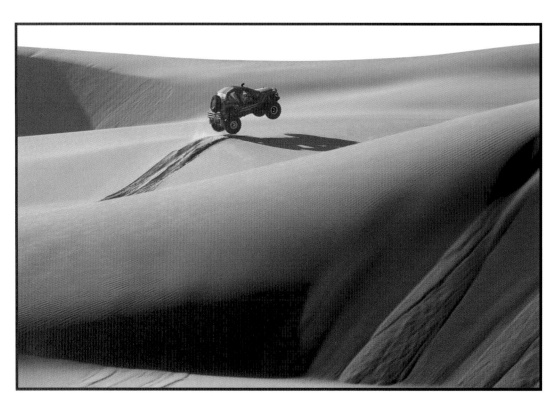

Showing off

could cause your downfall.

Upset the Board

and your career could end up here!

There'll always be someone waiting in the wings,

or lurking in the shadows.

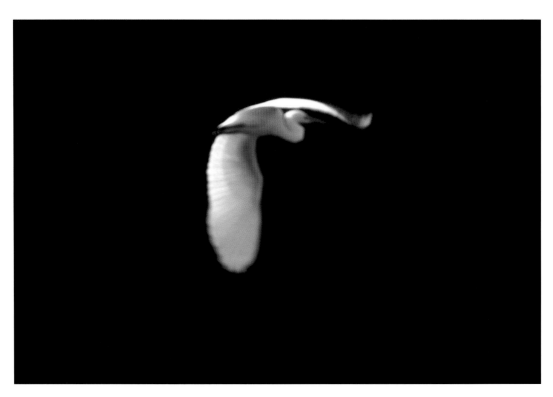

Don't flap,

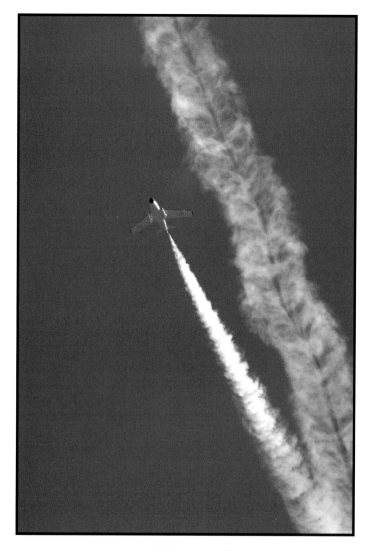

or you could veer off course.

Strive for peace

amid the chaos.

Follow your path

as far as you can.

When you've outgrown your environment,

head off in a new direction.

Lost?

Get back on track!

Burnt out?

Get professional help!

Putting all your eggs in one basket

could limit your opportunities.

It's not good to remain idle

… unless you're on a break.

Don't rest on your laurels,

reflecting on past glories.

If your career lies in ruins,

search for new opportunities.

A bright idea

is bound to strike.

Plan your course of action

before you attend a meeting.

If you meet with resistance,

try a different approach.

Looking for trouble?

You're bound to find it!

Left to paddle your own canoe?

Go for it!

You'll find your safe harbour one day,

and realise just how far you've come.

If you liked *Corporate Tricks* then you'll love *Soft Landings*.

Soft Landings

Margaret Polglase
Photography by Rob Henderson